The
CONSTITUTION
of the state of
MONTANA

The
CONSTITUTION
of the state of
MONTANA

as Adopted By the Constitutional Convention March 22, 1972,
and as Ratified By the People, June 6, 1972,
Referendum No. 68

Proseyr Publishing
Red Lodge, MT U.S.A.

The Constitution of the State of Montana

Book design by Gary D. Robson

Body copy set in Book Antiqua
Headings set in Franklin Gothic

ISBN 978-0-9659609-3-9
9 8 7 6 5 4 3 2

Proseyr Publishing
PO Box 1630, Red Lodge, MT 59068
www.proseyr.com

The text contained in this book is taken from Montana Code Annotated 2015, as published on the official Montana State website as of October of 2015. Except for headings, all capitalization and punctuation are as published by the state.

The most current version of the Montana state constitution can be found at

http://leg.mt.gov/bills/mca_toc/CONSTITUTION.htm

This book is intended only for reference and education for the citizens of Montana, and is not to be used for official legislative or judicial purposes.

Montana Fast Facts

Capital	Helena
Territory	May 26, 1864
Statehood	November 8, 1889 (Montana was the 41st state)
Size	Montana is the 4th largest state, with total land area of 147,040 square miles
Population	Estimated 1,023,579 at 2014 census
Motto	Oro y Plata ("Gold and Silver")

Official State Symbols

Animal	Grizzly Bear
Bird	Western Meadowlark
Butterfly	Mourning Cloak
Fish	Blackspotted Cutthroat Trout
Flower	Bitterroot
Fossil	Duck-Billed Dinosaur (*Maiasaura peeblesorum*)
Gemstones	Agate & Sapphire
Grass	Bluebunch Wheatgrass
Tree	Ponderosa Pine

Contents

Preamble 1
Article I. Compact With The United States 2
Article II. Declaration Of Rights 3
Article III. General Government 8
Article IV. Suffrage And Elections 10
Article V. The Legislature 12
Article VI. The Executive 16
Article VII. The Judiciary 21
Article VIII. Revenue And Finance 25
Article IX. Environment And Natural Resources 29
Article X. Education And Public Lands 31
Article XI. Local Government 35
Article XII. Departments And Institutions 38
Article XIII. General Provisions 40
Article XIV. Constitutional Revision 41
Transition Schedule 45

Preamble

We the people of Montana grateful to God for the quiet beauty of our state, the grandeur of our mountains, the vastness of our rolling plains, and desiring to improve the quality of life, equality of opportunity and to secure the blessings of liberty for this and future generations do ordain and establish this constitution.

Article I. Compact With The United States

All provisions of the enabling act of Congress (approved February 22, 1889, 25 Stat. 676), as amended and of Ordinance No. 1, appended to the Constitution of the state of Montana and approved February 22, 1889, including the agreement and declaration that all lands owned or held by any Indian or Indian tribes shall remain under the absolute jurisdiction and control of the congress of the United States, continue in full force and effect until revoked by the consent of the United States and the people of Montana.

Article II. Declaration Of Rights

Section 1. Popular sovereignty.
All political power is vested in and derived from the people. All government of right originates with the people, is founded upon their will only, and is instituted solely for the good of the whole.

Section 2. Self-government.
The people have the exclusive right of governing themselves as a free, sovereign, and independent state. They may alter or abolish the constitution and form of government whenever they deem it necessary.

Section 3. Inalienable rights.
All persons are born free and have certain inalienable rights. They include the right to a clean and healthful environment and the rights of pursuing life's basic necessities, enjoying and defending their lives and liberties, acquiring, possessing and protecting property, and seeking their safety, health and happiness in all lawful ways. In enjoying these rights, all persons recognize corresponding responsibilities.

Section 4. Individual dignity.
The dignity of the human being is inviolable. No person shall be denied the equal protection of the laws. Neither the state nor any person, firm, corporation, or institution shall discriminate against any person in the exercise of his civil or political rights on account of race, color, sex, culture, social origin or condition, or political or religious ideas.

Section 5. Freedom of religion.
The state shall make no law respecting an establishment of religion or prohibiting the free exercise thereof.

Section 6. Freedom of assembly.
The people shall have the right peaceably to assemble, petition for redress or peaceably protest governmental action.

Section 7. Freedom of speech, expression, and press.
No law shall be passed impairing the freedom of speech or expression. Every person shall be free to speak or publish whatever he will on any subject, being responsible for all abuse of that liberty. In all suits and prosecutions for libel or slander the truth thereof may be given in evidence; and the jury, under the direction of the court, shall determine the law and the facts.

Section 8. Right of participation.
The public has the right to expect governmental agencies to afford such reasonable opportunity for citizen participation in the operation of the agencies prior to the final decision as may be provided by law.

Section 9. Right to know.
No person shall be deprived of the right to examine documents or to observe the deliberations of all public bodies or agencies of state government and its subdivisions, except in cases in which the demand of individual privacy clearly exceeds the merits of public disclosure.

Section 10. Right of privacy.
The right of individual privacy is essential to the well-being of a free society and shall not be infringed without the showing of a compelling state interest.

Section 11. Searches and seizures.
The people shall be secure in their persons, papers, homes and effects from unreasonable searches and seizures. No warrant to search any place, or seize any person or thing shall issue without describing the place to be searched or the person or thing to be seized, or without probable cause, supported by oath or affirmation reduced to writing.

Section 12. Right to bear arms.
The right of any person to keep or bear arms in defense of his own home, person, and property, or in aid of the civil power when thereto legally summoned, shall not be called in question, but nothing herein contained shall be held to permit the carrying of concealed weapons.

Section 13. Right of suffrage.
All elections shall be free and open, and no power, civil or military, shall at any time interfere to prevent the free exercise of the right of suffrage.

Section 14. Adult rights.
A person 18 years of age or older is an adult for all purposes, except that the legislature or the people by initiative may establish the legal age for purchasing, consuming, or possessing alcoholic beverages.

Section 15. Rights of persons not adults.
The rights of persons under 18 years of age shall include, but not be limited to, all the fundamental rights of this Article unless specifically precluded by laws which enhance the protection of such persons.

History: Amd. Const. Amend. No. 4, approved Nov. 7, 1978; amd. Const. Amend. No. 16, approved Nov. 4, 1986.

Section 16. The administration of justice.
Courts of justice shall be open to every person, and speedy remedy afforded for every injury of person, property, or character. No person shall be deprived of this full legal redress for injury incurred in employment for which another person may be liable except as to fellow employees and his immediate employer who hired him if such immediate employer provides coverage under the Workmen's Compensation Laws of this state. Right and justice shall be administered without sale, denial, or delay.

Section 17. Due process of law.
No person shall be deprived of life, liberty, or property without due process of law.

Section 18. State subject to suit.
The state, counties, cities, towns, and all other local governmental entities shall have no immunity from suit for injury to a person or property, except as may be specifically provided by law by a 2/3 vote of each house of the legislature.

History: Amd. Const. Amend. No. 2, approved Nov. 5, 1974.

Section 19. Habeas corpus.
The privilege of the writ of habeas corpus shall never be suspended.

Section 20. Initiation of proceedings.
(1) Criminal offenses within the jurisdiction of any court inferior to the district court shall be prosecuted by complaint. All criminal actions in district court, except those on appeal, shall be prosecuted either by information, after examination and commitment by a magistrate or after leave granted by the court, or by indictment without such examination, commitment or leave.

(2) A grand jury shall consist of eleven persons, of whom eight must concur to find an indictment. A grand jury shall be drawn and summoned only at the discretion and order of the district judge.

Section 21. Bail.
All persons shall be bailable by sufficient sureties, except for capital offenses, when the proof is evident or the presumption great.

Section 22. Excessive sanctions.
Excessive bail shall not be required, or excessive fines imposed, or cruel and unusual punishments inflicted.

Section 23. Detention.
No person shall be imprisoned for the purpose of securing his testimony in any criminal proceeding longer than may be necessary in order to take his deposition. If he can give security for his appearance at the time of trial, he shall be discharged upon giving the same; if he cannot give security, his deposition shall be taken in the manner provided by law, and in the presence of the accused and his counsel, or without their presence, if they shall fail to attend the examination after reasonable notice of the time and place thereof.

Section 24. Rights of the accused.
In all criminal prosecutions the accused shall have the right to appear and defend in person and by counsel; to demand the nature and cause of the accusation; to meet the witnesses against him face to face; to have process to compel the attendance of witnesses in his behalf, and a speedy public trial by an impartial jury of the county or district in which the offense is alleged to have been committed, subject to the right of the state to have a change of venue for any of the causes for which the defendant may obtain the same.

Section 25. Self-incrimination and double jeopardy.
No person shall be compelled to testify against himself in a criminal proceeding. No person shall be again put in jeopardy for the same offense previously tried in any jurisdiction.

Section 26. Trial by jury.
The right of trial by jury is secured to all and shall remain inviolate. But upon default of appearance or by consent of the parties expressed in such manner as the law may provide, all cases may be tried without a jury or before fewer than the number of jurors provided by law. In all civil actions, two-thirds of the jury may render a verdict, and a verdict so rendered shall have the same force and effect as if all had concurred therein. In all criminal actions, the verdict shall be unanimous.

Section 27. Imprisonment for debt.
No person shall be imprisoned for debt except in the manner provided by law, upon refusal to deliver up his estate for the benefit of his creditors, or in cases of tort, where there is strong presumption of fraud.

Section 28. Criminal justice policy – rights of the convicted.
(1) Laws for the punishment of crime shall be founded on the principles of prevention, reformation, public safety, and restitution for victims.

(2) Full rights are restored by termination of state supervision for any offense against the state.

History: Amd. Const. Amend. No. 33, approved Nov. 3, 1998.

Section 29. Eminent domain.
Private property shall not be taken or damaged for public use without just compensation to the full extent of the loss having been first made to or paid into court for the owner. In the event of litigation, just compensation shall include necessary expenses of litigation to be awarded by the court when the private property owner prevails.

Section 30. Treason and descent of estates.
Treason against the state shall consist only in levying war against it, or in adhering to its enemies, giving them aid and comfort; no person shall be convicted of treason except on the testimony of two witnesses to the same overt act, or on his confession in open court; no person shall be attainted of treason or felony by the legislature; no conviction shall cause the loss of property to the relatives or heirs of the convicted. The estates of suicides shall descend or vest as in cases of natural death.

Section 31. Ex post facto, obligation of contracts, and irrevocable privileges.
No ex post facto law nor any law impairing the obligation of contracts, or making any irrevocable grant of special privileges, franchises, or immunities, shall be passed by the legislature.

Section 32. Civilian control of the military.
The military shall always be in strict subordination to the civil power; no soldier shall in time of peace be quartered in any house without the consent of the owner, nor in time of war, except in the manner provided by law.

Section 33. Importation of armed persons.
No armed person or persons or armed body of men shall be brought into this state for the preservation of the peace, or the suppression of domestic violence, except upon the application of the legislature, or of the governor when the legislature cannot be convened.

Section 34. Unenumerated rights.
The enumeration in this constitution of certain rights shall not be construed to deny, impair, or disparage others retained by the people.

Section 35. Servicemen, servicewomen, and veterans.
The people declare that Montana servicemen, servicewomen, and veterans may be given special considerations determined by the legislature.

Article III. General Government

Section 1. Separation of powers.
The power of the government of this state is divided into three distinct branches – legislative, executive, and judicial. No person or persons charged with the exercise of power properly belonging to one branch shall exercise any power properly belonging to either of the others, except as in this constitution expressly directed or permitted.

Section 2. Continuity of government.
The seat of government shall be in Helena, except during periods of emergency resulting from disasters or enemy attack. The legislature may enact laws to insure the continuity of government during a period of emergency without regard for other provisions of the constitution. They shall be effective only during the period of emergency that affects a particular office or governmental operation.

Section 3. Oath of office.
Members of the legislature and all executive, ministerial and judicial officers, shall take and subscribe the following oath or affirmation, before they enter upon the duties of their offices: "I do solemnly swear (or affirm) that I will support, protect and defend the constitution of the United States, and the constitution of the state of Montana, and that I will discharge the duties of my office with fidelity (so help me God)." No other oath, declaration, or test shall be required as a qualification for any office or public trust.

Section 4. Initiative.
(1) The people may enact laws by initiative on all matters except appropriations of money and local or special laws.

(2) Initiative petitions must contain the full text of the proposed measure, shall be signed by at least five percent of the qualified electors in each of at least one-half of the counties and the total number of signers must be at least five percent of the total qualified electors of the state. Petitions shall be filed with the secretary of state at least three months prior to the election at which the measure will be voted upon.

(3) The sufficiency of the initiative petition shall not be questioned after the election is held.

History: Amd. Const. Amend. No. 38, approved Nov. 5, 2002.

Section 5. Referendum.
(1) The people may approve or reject by referendum any act of the legislature except an appropriation of money. A referendum shall be held either upon order by the legislature or upon petition signed by at least five percent of the qualified electors in each of at least one-third of the legislative representative districts. The total number of signers must be at least five percent of the qualified electors of the state. A referendum petition shall be filed with the secretary of state no later than six months after adjournment of the legislature which passed the act.

(2) An act referred to the people is in effect until suspended by petitions signed by at least 15 percent of the qualified electors in a majority of the legislative representative districts. If so suspended the act shall become operative only after it is approved at an election, the result of which has been determined and declared as provided by law.

Section 6. Elections.
The people shall vote on initiative and referendum measures at the general election unless the legislature orders a special election.

Section 7. Number of electors.
(1) The number of qualified electors required in each legislative representative district and in the state shall be determined by the number of votes cast for the office of governor in the preceding general election.

(2) For the purposes of a constitutional amendment, the number of qualified electors in each county and in the state shall be determined by the number of votes cast for the office of governor in the preceding general election.

(3) For the purposes of a statutory initiative, the number of qualified electors required in each county and in the state shall be determined by the number of votes cast for the office of governor in the preceding general election.

History: Amd. Const. Amend. No. 37, approved Nov. 5, 2002; amd. Const. Amend. No. 38, approved Nov. 5, 2002.

Section 8. Prohibition.
The provisions of this Article do not apply to CONSTITUTIONAL REVISION, Article XIV.

Section 9. Gambling.
All forms of gambling, lotteries, and gift enterprises are prohibited unless authorized by acts of the legislature or by the people through initiative or referendum.

Article IV. Suffrage And Elections

Section 1. Ballot.
All elections by the people shall be by secret ballot.

Section 2. Qualified elector.
Any citizen of the United States 18 years of age or older who meets the registration and residence requirements provided by law is a qualified elector unless he is serving a sentence for a felony in a penal institution or is of unsound mind, as determined by a court.

Section 3. Elections.
The legislature shall provide by law the requirements for residence, registration, absentee voting, and administration of elections. It may provide for a system of poll booth registration, and shall insure the purity of elections and guard against abuses of the electoral process.

Section 4. Eligibility for public office.
Any qualified elector is eligible to any public office except as otherwise provided in this constitution. The legislature may provide additional qualifications but no person convicted of a felony shall be eligible to hold office until his final discharge from state supervision.

Section 5. Result of elections.
In all elections held by the people, the person or persons receiving the largest number of votes shall be declared elected.

Section 6. Privilege from arrest.
A qualified elector is privileged from arrest at polling places and in going to and returning therefrom, unless apprehended in the commission of a felony or a breach of the peace.

Section 7. Ballot issues – challenges – elections.
(1) An initiative or referendum that qualifies for the ballot under Article III or Article XIV shall be submitted to the qualified electors as provided in the Article under which the initiative or referendum qualified unless a new election is held pursuant to this section.

(2) A preelection challenge to the procedure by which an initiative or referendum qualified for the ballot or a postelection challenge to the manner in which the election was conducted shall be given priority by the courts.

(3) If the election on an initiative or referendum properly qualifying for the ballot is declared invalid because the election was improperly conducted, the secretary of state shall submit the issue to the qualified electors at the next regularly scheduled statewide election unless the legislature orders a special election.

History: En. Sec. 1, Const. Amend. No. 21, approved Nov. 6, 1990.

Section 8. Limitation on terms of office.

(1) The secretary of state or other authorized official shall not certify a candidate's nomination or election to, or print or cause to be printed on any ballot the name of a candidate for, one of the following offices if, at the end of the current term of that office, the candidate will have served in that office or had he not resigned or been recalled would have served in that office:

   (a) 8 or more years in any 16-year period as governor, lieutenant governor, secretary of state, state auditor, attorney general, or superintendent of public instruction;

   (b) 8 or more years in any 16-year period as a state representative;

   (c) 8 or more years in any 16-year period as a state senator;

   (d) 6 or more years in any 12-year period as a member of the U.S. house of representatives; and

   (e) 12 or more years in any 24-year period as a member of the U.S. senate.

(2) When computing time served for purposes of subsection (1), the provisions of subsection (1) do not apply to time served in terms that end during or prior to January 1993.

(3) Nothing contained herein shall preclude an otherwise qualified candidate from being certified as nominated or elected by virtue of write-in votes cast for said candidate.

History: En. Sec. 1, Const. Initiative No. 64, approved Nov. 3, 1992.

Article V. The Legislature

Section 1. Power and structure.
The legislative power is vested in a legislature consisting of a senate and a house of representatives. The people reserve to themselves the powers of initiative and referendum.

Section 2. Size.
The size of the legislature shall be provided by law, but the senate shall not have more than 50 or fewer than 40 members and the house shall not have more than 100 or fewer than 80 members.

Section 3. Election and terms.
A member of the house of representatives shall be elected for a term of two years and a member of the senate for a term of four years each to begin on a date provided by law. One-half of the senators shall be elected every two years.

Section 4. Qualifications.
A candidate for the legislature shall be a resident of the state for at least one year next preceding the general election. For six months next preceding the general election, he shall be a resident of the county if it contains one or more districts or of the district if it contains all or parts of more than one county.

Section 5. Compensation.
Each member of the legislature shall receive compensation for his services and allowances provided by law. No legislature may fix its own compensation.

Section 6. Sessions.
The legislature shall meet each odd-numbered year in regular session of not more than 90 legislative days. Any legislature may increase the limit on the length of any subsequent session. The legislature may be convened in special sessions by the governor or at the written request of a majority of the members.

History: Amd. Const. Initiative No. 1, approved Nov. 5, 1974.

Section 7. Vacancies.
A vacancy in the legislature shall be filled by special election for the unexpired term unless otherwise provided by law.

Section 8. Immunity.
A member of the legislature is privileged from arrest during attendance at sessions of the legislature and in going to and returning therefrom, unless apprehended in the

commission of a felony or a breach of the peace. He shall not be questioned in any other place for any speech or debate in the legislature.

Section 9. Disqualification.
No member of the legislature shall, during the term for which he shall have been elected, be appointed to any civil office under the state; and no member of congress, or other person holding an office (except notary public, or the militia) under the United States or this state, shall be a member of the legislature during his continuance in office.

Section 10. Organization and procedure.
(1) Each house shall judge the election and qualifications of its members. It may by law vest in the courts the power to try and determine contested elections. Each house shall choose its officers from among its members, keep a journal, and make rules for its proceedings. Each house may expel or punish a member for good cause shown with the concurrence of two-thirds of all its members.

(2) A majority of each house constitutes a quorum. A smaller number may adjourn from day to day and compel attendance of absent members.

(3) The sessions of the legislature and of the committee of the whole, all committee meetings, and all hearings shall be open to the public.

(4) The legislature may establish a legislative council and other interim committees. The legislature shall establish a legislative post-audit committee which shall supervise post-auditing duties provided by law.

(5) Neither house shall, without the consent of the other, adjourn or recess for more than three days or to any place other than that in which the two houses are sitting.

Section 11. Bills.
(1) A law shall be passed by bill which shall not be so altered or amended on its passage through the legislature as to change its original purpose. No bill shall become law except by a vote of the majority of all members present and voting.

(2) Every vote of each member of the legislature on each substantive question in the legislature, in any committee, or in committee of the whole shall be recorded and made public. On final passage, the vote shall be taken by ayes and noes and the names entered on the journal.

(3) Each bill, except general appropriation bills and bills for the codification and general revision of the laws, shall contain only one subject, clearly expressed in its title. If any subject is embraced in any act and is not expressed in the title, only so much of the act not so expressed is void.

(4) A general appropriation bill shall contain only appropriations for the ordinary expenses of the legislative, executive, and judicial branches, for interest on the public debt, and for public schools. Every other appropriation shall be made by a separate bill, containing but one subject.

(5) No appropriation shall be made for religious, charitable, industrial, educational, or benevolent purposes to any private individual, private association, or private corporation not under control of the state.

(6) A law may be challenged on the ground of noncompliance with this section only within two years after its effective date.

Section 12. Local and special legislation.

The legislature shall not pass a special or local act when a general act is, or can be made, applicable.

Section 13. Impeachment.

(1) The governor, executive officers, heads of state departments, judicial officers, and such other officers as may be provided by law are subject to impeachment, and upon conviction shall be removed from office. Other proceedings for removal from public office for cause may be provided by law.

(2) The legislature shall provide for the manner, procedure, and causes for impeachment and may select the senate as tribunal.

(3) Impeachment shall be brought only by a two-thirds vote of the house. The tribunal hearing the charges shall convict only by a vote of two-thirds or more of its members.

(4) Conviction shall extend only to removal from office, but the party, whether convicted or acquitted, shall also be liable to prosecution according to law.

Section 14. Districting and apportionment.

(1) The state shall be divided into as many districts as there are members of the house, and each district shall elect one representative. Each senate district shall be composed of two adjoining house districts, and shall elect one senator. Each district shall consist of compact and contiguous territory. All districts shall be as nearly equal in population as is practicable.

(2) In the legislative session following ratification of this constitution and thereafter in each session preceding each federal population census, a commission of five citizens, none of whom may be public officials, shall be selected to prepare a plan for redistricting and reapportioning the state into legislative districts and a plan for redistricting the state into congressional districts. The majority and minority leaders of each house shall each designate one commissioner. Within 20 days

after their designation, the four commissioners shall select the fifth member, who shall serve as chairman of the commission. If the four members fail to select the fifth member within the time prescribed, a majority of the supreme court shall select him.

(3) Within 90 days after the official final decennial census figures are available, the commission shall file its final plan for congressional districts with the secretary of state and it shall become law.

(4) The commission shall submit its plan for legislative districts to the legislature at the first regular session after its appointment or after the census figures are available. Within 30 days after submission, the legislature shall return the plan to the commission with its recommendations. Within 30 days thereafter, the commission shall file its final plan for legislative districts with the secretary of state and it shall become law.

(5) Upon filing both plans, the commission is then dissolved.

History: Amd. Const. Amend. No. 14, approved Nov. 6, 1984.

Article VI. The Executive

Section 1. Officers.
(1) The executive branch includes a governor, lieutenant governor, secretary of state, attorney general, superintendent of public instruction, and auditor.

(2) Each holds office for a term of four years which begins on the first Monday of January next succeeding election, and until a successor is elected and qualified.

(3) Each shall reside at the seat of government, there keep the public records of his office, and perform such other duties as are provided in this constitution and by law.

Section 2. Election.
(1) The governor, lieutenant governor, secretary of state, attorney general, superintendent of public instruction, and auditor shall be elected by the qualified electors at a general election provided by law.

(2) Each candidate for governor shall file jointly with a candidate for lieutenant governor in primary elections, or so otherwise comply with nomination procedures provided by law that the offices of governor and lieutenant governor are voted upon together in primary and general elections.

Section 3. Qualifications.
(1) No person shall be eligible to the office of governor, lieutenant governor, secretary of state, attorney general, superintendent of public instruction, or auditor unless he is 25 years of age or older at the time of his election. In addition, each shall be a citizen of the United States who has resided within the state two years next preceding his election.

(2) Any person with the foregoing qualifications is eligible to the office of attorney general if an attorney in good standing admitted to practice law in Montana who has engaged in the active practice thereof for at least five years before election.

(3) The superintendent of public instruction shall have such educational qualifications as are provided by law.

Section 4. Duties.
(1) The executive power is vested in the governor who shall see that the laws are faithfully executed. He shall have such other duties as are provided in this constitution and by law.

(2) The lieutenant governor shall perform the duties provided by law and those delegated to him by the governor. No power specifically vested in the governor by this constitution may be delegated to the lieutenant governor.

(3) The secretary of state shall maintain official records of the executive branch and of the acts of the legislature, as provided by law. He shall keep the great seal of the state of Montana and perform any other duties provided by law.

(4) The attorney general is the legal officer of the state and shall have the duties and powers provided by law.

(5) The superintendent of public instruction and the auditor shall have such duties as are provided by law.

Section 5. Compensation.

(1) Officers of the executive branch shall receive salaries provided by law.

(2) During his term, no elected officer of the executive branch may hold another public office or receive compensation for services from any other governmental agency. He may be a candidate for any public office during his term.

Section 6. Vacancy in office.

(1) If the office of lieutenant governor becomes vacant by his succession to the office of governor, or by his death, resignation, or disability as determined by law, the governor shall appoint a qualified person to serve in that office for the remainder of the term. If both the elected governor and the elected lieutenant governor become unable to serve in the office of governor, succession to the respective offices shall be as provided by law for the period until the next general election. Then, a governor and lieutenant governor shall be elected to fill the remainder of the original term.

(2) If the office of secretary of state, attorney general, auditor, or superintendent of public instruction becomes vacant by death, resignation, or disability as determined by law, the governor shall appoint a qualified person to serve in that office until the next general election and until a successor is elected and qualified. The person elected to fill a vacancy shall hold the office until the expiration of the term for which his predecessor was elected.

Section 7. 20 departments.

All executive and administrative offices, boards, bureaus, commissions, agencies and instrumentalities of the executive branch (except for the office of governor, lieutenant governor, secretary of state, attorney general, superintendent of public instruction, and auditor) and their respective functions, powers, and duties, shall be allocated by law among not more than 20 principal departments so as to provide an orderly arrangement in the administrative organization of state government. Temporary commissions may be established by law and need not be allocated within a department.

Section 8. Appointing power.

(1) The departments provided for in section 7 shall be under the supervision of the governor. Except as otherwise provided in this constitution or by law, each department shall be headed by a single executive appointed by the governor subject to confirmation by the senate to hold office until the end of the governor's term unless sooner removed by the governor.

(2) The governor shall appoint, subject to confirmation by the senate, all officers provided for in this constitution or by law whose appointment or election is not otherwise provided for. They shall hold office until the end of the governor's term unless sooner removed by the governor.

(3) If a vacancy occurs in any such office when the legislature is not in session, the governor shall appoint a qualified person to discharge the duties thereof until the office is filled by appointment and confirmation.

(4) A person not confirmed by the senate for an office shall not, except at its request, be nominated again for that office at the same session, or be appointed to that office when the legislature is not in session.

Section 9. Budget and messages.

The governor shall at the beginning of each legislative session, and may at other times, give the legislature information and recommend measures he considers necessary. The governor shall submit to the legislature at a time fixed by law, a budget for the ensuing fiscal period setting forth in detail for all operating funds the proposed expenditures and estimated revenue of the state.

Section 10. Veto power.

(1) Each bill passed by the legislature, except bills proposing amendments to the Montana constitution, bills ratifying proposed amendments to the United States constitution, resolutions, and initiative and referendum measures, shall be submitted to the governor for his signature. If he does not sign or veto the bill within 10 days after its delivery to him, it shall become law. The governor shall return a vetoed bill to the legislature with a statement of his reasons therefor.

(2) The governor may return any bill to the legislature with his recommendation for amendment. If the legislature passes the bill in accordance with the governor's recommendation, it shall again return the bill to the governor for his reconsideration. The governor shall not return a bill for amendment a second time.

(3) If after receipt of a veto message, two-thirds of the members of each house present approve the bill, it shall become law.

(4)

(a) If the legislature is not in session when the governor vetoes a bill approved by two-thirds of the members present, he shall return the bill with his reasons therefor to the secretary of state. The secretary of state shall poll the members of the legislature by mail and shall send each member a copy of the governor's veto message. If two-thirds or more of the members of each house vote to override the veto, the bill shall become law.

(b) The legislature may reconvene as provided by law to reconsider any bill vetoed by the governor when the legislature is not in session.

(5) The governor may veto items in appropriation bills, and in such instances the procedure shall be the same as upon veto of an entire bill.

History: Amd. Const. Amend. No. 12, approved Nov. 2, 1982; amd. Const. Amend. No. 26, approved Nov. 8, 1994.

Section 11. Special session.

Whenever the governor considers it in the public interest, he may convene the legislature.

Section 12. Pardons.

The governor may grant reprieves, commutations and pardons, restore citizenship, and suspend and remit fines and forfeitures subject to procedures provided by law.

Section 13. Militia.

(1) The governor is commander-in-chief of the militia forces of the state, except when they are in the actual service of the United States. He may call out any part or all of the forces to aid in the execution of the laws, suppress insurrection, repel invasion, or protect life and property in natural disasters.

(2) The militia forces shall consist of all able-bodied citizens of the state except those exempted by law.

Section 14. Succession.

(1) If the governor-elect is disqualified or dies, the lieutenant governor-elect upon qualifying for the office shall become governor for the full term. If the governor-elect fails to assume office for any other reason, the lieutenant governor-elect upon qualifying as such shall serve as acting governor until the governor-elect is able to assume office, or until the office becomes vacant.

(2) The lieutenant governor shall serve as acting governor when so requested in writing by the governor. After the governor has been absent from the state for more than 45 consecutive days, the lieutenant governor shall serve as acting governor.

(3) He shall serve as acting governor when the governor is so disabled as to be unable to communicate to the lieutenant governor the fact of his inability to perform the duties of his office. The lieutenant governor shall continue to serve as acting governor until the governor is able to resume the duties of his office.

(4) Whenever, at any other time, the lieutenant governor and attorney general transmit to the legislature their written declaration that the governor is unable to discharge the powers and duties of his office, the legislature shall convene to determine whether he is able to do so.

(5) If the legislature, within 21 days after convening, determines by two-thirds vote of its members that the governor is unable to discharge the powers and duties of his office, the lieutenant governor shall serve as acting governor. Thereafter, when the governor transmits to the legislature his written declaration that no inability exists, he shall resume the powers and duties of his office within 15 days, unless the legislature determines otherwise by two-thirds vote of its members. If the legislature so determines, the lieutenant governor shall continue to serve as acting governor.

(6) If the office of governor becomes vacant by reason of death, resignation, or disqualification, the lieutenant governor shall become governor for the remainder of the term, except as provided in this constitution.

(7) Additional succession to fill vacancies shall be provided by law.

(8) When there is a vacancy in the office of governor, the successor shall be the governor. The acting governor shall have the powers and duties of the office of governor only for the period during which he serves.

Section 15. Information for governor.

(1) The governor may require information in writing, under oath when required, from the officers of the executive branch upon any subject relating to the duties of their respective offices.

(2) He may require information in writing, under oath, from all officers and managers of state institutions.

(3) He may appoint a committee to investigate and report to him upon the condition of any executive office or state institution.

Article VII. The Judiciary

Section 1. Judicial power.
The judicial power of the state is vested in one supreme court, district courts, justice courts, and such other courts as may be provided by law.

Section 2. Supreme court jurisdiction.
(1) The supreme court has appellate jurisdiction and may issue, hear, and determine writs appropriate thereto. It has original jurisdiction to issue, hear, and determine writs of habeas corpus and such other writs as may be provided by law.

(2) It has general supervisory control over all other courts.

(3) It may make rules governing appellate procedure, practice and procedure for all other courts, admission to the bar and the conduct of its members. Rules of procedure shall be subject to disapproval by the legislature in either of the two sessions following promulgation.

(4) Supreme court process shall extend to all parts of the state.

Section 3. Supreme court organization.
(1) The supreme court consists of one chief justice and four justices, but the legislature may increase the number of justices from four to six. A majority shall join in and pronounce decisions, which must be in writing.

(2) A district judge shall be substituted for the chief justice or a justice in the event of disqualification or disability, and the opinion of the district judge sitting with the supreme court shall have the same effect as an opinion of a justice.

Section 4. District court jurisdiction.
(1) The district court has original jurisdiction in all criminal cases amounting to felony and all civil matters and cases at law and in equity. It may issue all writs appropriate to its jurisdiction. It shall have the power of naturalization and such additional jurisdiction as may be delegated by the laws of the United States or the state of Montana. Its process shall extend to all parts of the state.

(2) The district court shall hear appeals from inferior courts as trials anew unless otherwise provided by law. The legislature may provide for direct review by the district court of decisions of administrative agencies.

(3) Other courts may have jurisdiction of criminal cases not amounting to felony and such jurisdiction concurrent with that of the district court as may be provided by law.

Section 5. Justices of the peace.
(1) There shall be elected in each county at least one justice of the peace with qualifications, training, and monthly compensation provided by law. There shall be provided such facilities that they may perform their duties in dignified surroundings.

(2) Justice courts shall have such original jurisdiction as may be provided by law. They shall not have trial jurisdiction in any criminal case designated a felony except as examining courts.

(3) The legislature may provide for additional justices of the peace in each county.

Section 6. Judicial districts.
(1) The legislature shall divide the state into judicial districts and provide for the number of judges in each district. Each district shall be formed of compact territory and be bounded by county lines.

(2) The legislature may change the number and boundaries of judicial districts and the number of judges in each district, but no change in boundaries or the number of districts or judges therein shall work a removal of any judge from office during the term for which he was elected or appointed.

(3) The chief justice may, upon request of the district judge, assign district judges and other judges for temporary service from one district to another, and from one county to another.

Section 7. Terms and pay.
(1) All justices and judges shall be paid as provided by law, but salaries shall not be diminished during terms of office.

(2) Terms of office shall be eight years for supreme court justices, six years for district court judges, four years for justices of the peace, and as provided by law for other judges.

Section 8. Selection.
(1) Supreme court justices and district court judges shall be elected by the qualified electors as provided by law.

(2) For any vacancy in the office of supreme court justice or district court judge, the governor shall appoint a replacement from nominees selected in the manner provided by law. If the governor fails to appoint within thirty days after receipt of nominees, the chief justice or acting chief justice shall make the appointment from the same nominees within thirty days of the governor's failure to appoint. Appointments made under this subsection shall be subject to confirmation by the senate, as provided by law. If the appointee is not confirmed, the office shall be

vacant and a replacement shall be made under the procedures provided for in this section. The appointee shall serve until the election for the office as provided by law and until a successor is elected and qualified. The person elected or retained at the election shall serve until the expiration of the term for which his predecessor was elected. No appointee, whether confirmed or unconfirmed, shall serve past the term of his predecessor without standing for election.

(3) If an incumbent files for election and there is no election contest for the office, the name of the incumbent shall nevertheless be placed on the general election ballot to allow the voters of the state or district to approve or reject him. If an incumbent is rejected, the vacancy in the office for which the election was held shall be filled as provided in subsection (2).

History: Amd. Const. Amend. No. 22, approved Nov. 3, 1992.

Section 9. Qualifications.

(1) A citizen of the United States who has resided in the state two years immediately before taking office is eligible to the office of supreme court justice or district court judge if admitted to the practice of law in Montana for at least five years prior to the date of appointment or election. Qualifications and methods of selection of judges of other courts shall be provided by law.

(2) No supreme court justice or district court judge shall solicit or receive compensation in any form whatever on account of his office, except salary and actual necessary travel expense.

(3) Except as otherwise provided in this constitution, no supreme court justice or district court judge shall practice law during his term of office, engage in any other employment for which salary or fee is paid, or hold office in a political party.

(4) Supreme court justices shall reside within the state. During his term of office, a district court judge shall reside in the district and a justice of the peace shall reside in the county in which he is elected or appointed. The residency requirement for every other judge must be provided by law.

History: Amd. Const. Amend. No. 19, approved Nov. 8, 1988.

Section 10. Forfeiture of judicial position.

Any holder of a judicial position forfeits that position by either filing for an elective public office other than a judicial position or absenting himself from the state for more than 60 consecutive days.

Section 11. Removal and discipline.

(1) The legislature shall create a judicial standards commission consisting of five persons and provide for the appointment thereto of two district judges, one attorney, and two citizens who are neither judges nor attorneys.

(2) The commission shall investigate complaints, and make rules implementing this section. It may subpoena witnesses and documents.

(3) Upon recommendation of the commission, the supreme court may:

   (a) Retire any justice or judge for disability that seriously interferes with the performance of his duties and is or may become permanent; or

   (b) Censure, suspend, or remove any justice or judge for willful misconduct in office, willful and persistent failure to perform his duties, violation of canons of judicial ethics adopted by the supreme court of the state of Montana, or habitual intemperance.

(4) The proceedings of the commission are confidential except as provided by statute.

History: Amd. Const. Amend. No. 9, approved Nov. 4, 1980; amd. Const. Amend. No. 13, approved Nov. 6, 1984.

Article VIII. Revenue And Finance

Section 1. Tax purposes.
Taxes shall be levied by general laws for public purposes.

Section 2. Tax power inalienable.
The power to tax shall never be surrendered, suspended, or contracted away.

Section 3. Property tax administration.
The state shall appraise, assess, and equalize the valuation of all property which is to be taxed in the manner provided by law.

Section 4. Equal valuation.
All taxing jurisdictions shall use the assessed valuation of property established by the state.

Section 5. Property tax exemptions.
(1) The legislature may exempt from taxation:

   (a) Property of the United States, the state, counties, cities, towns, school districts, municipal corporations, and public libraries, but any private interest in such property may be taxed separately.

   (b) Institutions of purely public charity, hospitals and places of burial not used or held for private or corporate profit, places for actual religious worship, and property used exclusively for educational purposes.

   (c) Any other classes of property.

(2) The legislature may authorize creation of special improvement districts for capital improvements and the maintenance thereof. It may authorize the assessment of charges for such improvements and maintenance against tax exempt property directly benefited thereby.

Section 6. Highway revenue non-diversion.
(1) Revenue from gross vehicle weight fees and excise and license taxes (except general sales and use taxes) on gasoline, fuel, and other energy sources used to propel vehicles on public highways shall be used as authorized by the legislature, after deduction of statutory refunds and adjustments, solely for:

   (a) Payment of obligations incurred for construction, reconstruction, repair, operation, and maintenance of public highways, streets, roads, and bridges.

   (b) Payment of county, city, and town obligations on streets, roads, and bridges.

(c) Enforcement of highway safety, driver education, tourist promotion, and administrative collection costs.

(2) Such revenue may be appropriated for other purposes by a three-fifths vote of the members of each house of the legislature.

Section 7. Tax appeals.

The legislature shall provide independent appeal procedures for taxpayer grievances about appraisals, assessments, equalization, and taxes. The legislature shall include a review procedure at the local government unit level.

Section 8. State debt.

No state debt shall be created unless authorized by a two-thirds vote of the members of each house of the legislature or a majority of the electors voting thereon. No state debt shall be created to cover deficits incurred because appropriations exceeded anticipated revenue.

Section 9. Balanced budget.

Appropriations by the legislature shall not exceed anticipated revenue.

Section 10. Local government debt.

The legislature shall by law limit debts of counties, cities, towns, and all other local governmental entities.

Section 11. Use of loan proceeds.

All money borrowed by or on behalf of the state or any county, city, town, or other local governmental entity shall be used only for purposes specified in the authorizing law.

Section 12. Strict accountability.

The legislature shall by law insure strict accountability of all revenue received and money spent by the state and counties, cities, towns, and all other local governmental entities.

Section 13. Investment of public funds and public retirement system and state compensation insurance fund assets.

(1) The legislature shall provide for a unified investment program for public funds and public retirement system and state compensation insurance fund assets and provide rules therefor, including supervision of investment of surplus funds of all counties, cities, towns, and other local governmental entities. Each fund forming a part of the unified investment program shall be separately identified. Except as provided in subsections (3) and (4), no public funds shall be invested in

private corporate capital stock. The investment program shall be audited at least annually and a report thereof submitted to the governor and legislature.

(2) The public school fund and the permanent funds of the Montana university system and all other state institutions of learning shall be safely and conservatively invested in:

   (a) Public securities of the state, its subdivisions, local government units, and districts within the state, or

   (b) Bonds of the United States or other securities fully guaranteed as to principal and interest by the United States, or

   (c) Such other safe investments bearing a fixed rate of interest as may be provided by law.

(3) Investment of public retirement system assets shall be managed in a fiduciary capacity in the same manner that a prudent expert acting in a fiduciary capacity and familiar with the circumstances would use in the conduct of an enterprise of a similar character with similar aims. Public retirement system assets may be invested in private corporate capital stock.

(4) Investment of state compensation insurance fund assets shall be managed in a fiduciary capacity in the same manner that a prudent expert acting in a fiduciary capacity and familiar with the circumstances would use in the conduct of a private insurance organization. State compensation insurance fund assets may be invested in private corporate capital stock. However, the stock investments shall not exceed 25 percent of the book value of the state compensation insurance fund's total invested assets.

History: Amd. Const. Amend. No. 25, approved Nov. 8, 1994; amd. Const. Amend. No. 34, approved Nov. 7, 2000.

Section 14. Prohibited payments.

Except for interest on the public debt, no money shall be paid out of the treasury unless upon an appropriation made by law and a warrant drawn by the proper officer in pursuance thereof.

Section 15. Public retirement system assets.

(1) Public retirement systems shall be funded on an actuarially sound basis. Public retirement system assets, including income and actuarially required contributions, shall not be encumbered, diverted, reduced, or terminated and shall be held in trust to provide benefits to participants and their beneficiaries and to defray administrative expenses.

(2) The governing boards of public retirement systems shall administer the system, including actuarial determinations, as fiduciaries of system participants and their beneficiaries.

History: En. Sec. 2, Const. Amend. No. 25, approved Nov. 8, 1994.

Section 16. Limitation on sales tax or use tax rates.

The rate of a general statewide sales tax or use tax may not exceed 4%.

History: En. Sec. 1, Const. Amend. No. 27, approved Nov. 8, 1994.

Section 17. Prohibition on real property transfer taxes.

The state or any local government unit may not impose any tax, including a sales tax, on the sale or transfer of real property.

History: En. Sec. 1, Const. Initiative No. 105, approved Nov. 2, 2010.

Article IX. Environment And Natural Resources

Section 1. Protection and improvement.
(1) The state and each person shall maintain and improve a clean and healthful environment in Montana for present and future generations.
(2) The legislature shall provide for the administration and enforcement of this duty.
(3) The legislature shall provide adequate remedies for the protection of the environmental life support system from degradation and provide adequate remedies to prevent unreasonable depletion and degradation of natural resources.

Section 2. Reclamation.
(1) All lands disturbed by the taking of natural resources shall be reclaimed. The legislature shall provide effective requirements and standards for the reclamation of lands disturbed.
(2) The legislature shall provide for a fund, to be known as the resource indemnity trust of the state of Montana, to be funded by such taxes on the extraction of natural resources as the legislature may from time to time impose for that purpose.
(3) The principal of the resource indemnity trust shall forever remain inviolate in an amount of one hundred million dollars ($100,000,000), guaranteed by the state against loss or diversion.

History: Amd. Const. Amend. No. 1, approved Nov. 5, 1974.

Section 3. Water rights.
(1) All existing rights to the use of any waters for any useful or beneficial purpose are hereby recognized and confirmed.
(2) The use of all water that is now or may hereafter be appropriated for sale, rent, distribution, or other beneficial use, the right of way over the lands of others for all ditches, drains, flumes, canals, and aqueducts necessarily used in connection therewith, and the sites for reservoirs necessary for collecting and storing water shall be held to be a public use.
(3) All surface, underground, flood, and atmospheric waters within the boundaries of the state are the property of the state for the use of its people and are subject to appropriation for beneficial uses as provided by law.
(4) The legislature shall provide for the administration, control, and regulation of water rights and shall establish a system of centralized records, in addition to the present system of local records.

Section 4. Cultural resources.

The legislature shall provide for the identification, acquisition, restoration, enhancement, preservation, and administration of scenic, historic, archeologic, scientific, cultural, and recreational areas, sites, records and objects, and for their use and enjoyment by the people.

Section 5. Severance tax on coal — trust fund.

The legislature shall dedicate not less than one-fourth (1/4) of the coal severance tax to a trust fund, the interest and income from which may be appropriated. The principal of the trust shall forever remain inviolate unless appropriated by vote of three-fourths (3/4) of the members of each house of the legislature. After December 31, 1979, at least fifty percent (50%) of the severance tax shall be dedicated to the trust fund.

History: En. Sec. 1, Const. Amend. No. 3, approved Nov. 2, 1976.

Section 6. Noxious weed management trust fund.

(1) The legislature shall provide for a fund, to be known as the noxious weed management trust of the state of Montana, to be funded as provided by law.

(2) The principal of the noxious weed management trust fund shall forever remain inviolate in an amount of ten million dollars ($10,000,000) unless appropriated by vote of three-fourths (3/4) of the members of each house of the legislature.

(3) The interest and income generated from the noxious weed management trust fund may be appropriated by a majority vote of each house of the legislature. Appropriations of the interest and income shall be used only to fund the noxious weed management program, as provided by law.

(4) The principal of the noxious weed management trust fund in excess of ten million dollars ($10,000,000) may be appropriated by a majority vote of each house of the legislature. Appropriations of the principal in excess of ten million dollars ($10,000,000) shall be used only to fund the noxious weed management program, as provided by law.

History: En. Sec. 1, Const. Amend. No. 40, approved Nov. 2, 2004.

Section 7. Preservation of harvest heritage.

The opportunity to harvest wild fish and wild game animals is a heritage that shall forever be preserved to the individual citizens of the state and does not create a right to trespass on private property or diminution of other private rights.

History: En. Sec. 1, Const. Amend. No. 41, approved Nov. 2, 2004.

Article X. Education And Public Lands

Section 1. Educational goals and duties.
(1) It is the goal of the people to establish a system of education which will develop the full educational potential of each person. Equality of educational opportunity is guaranteed to each person of the state.

(2) The state recognizes the distinct and unique cultural heritage of the American Indians and is committed in its educational goals to the preservation of their cultural integrity.

(3) The legislature shall provide a basic system of free quality public elementary and secondary schools. The legislature may provide such other educational institutions, public libraries, and educational programs as it deems desirable. It shall fund and distribute in an equitable manner to the school districts the state's share of the cost of the basic elementary and secondary school system.

Section 2. Public school fund.
The public school fund of the state shall consist of:

(1) Proceeds from the school lands which have been or may hereafter be granted by the United States,

(2) Lands granted in lieu thereof,

(3) Lands given or granted by any person or corporation under any law or grant of the United States,

(4) All other grants of land or money made from the United States for general educational purposes or without special purpose,

(5) All interests in estates that escheat to the state,

(6) All unclaimed shares and dividends of any corporation incorporated in the state,

(7) All other grants, gifts, devises or bequests made to the state for general educational purposes.

Section 3. Public school fund inviolate.
The public school fund shall forever remain inviolate, guaranteed by the state against loss or diversion.

Section 4. Board of land commissioners.
The governor, superintendent of public instruction, auditor, secretary of state, and attorney general constitute the board of land commissioners. It has the authority to direct, control, lease, exchange, and sell school lands and lands which have been or

may be granted for the support and benefit of the various state educational institutions, under such regulations and restrictions as may be provided by law.

Section 5. Public school fund revenue.

(1) Ninety-five percent of all the interest received on the public school fund and ninety-five percent of all rent received from the leasing of school lands and all other income from the public school fund shall be equitably apportioned annually to public elementary and secondary school districts as provided by law.

(2) The remaining five percent of all interest received on the public school fund, and the remaining five percent of all rent received from the leasing of school lands and all other income from the public school fund shall annually be added to the public school fund and become and forever remain an inseparable and inviolable part thereof.

Section 6. Aid prohibited to sectarian schools.

(1) The legislature, counties, cities, towns, school districts, and public corporations shall not make any direct or indirect appropriation or payment from any public fund or monies, or any grant of lands or other property for any sectarian purpose or to aid any church, school, academy, seminary, college, university, or other literary or scientific institution, controlled in whole or in part by any church, sect, or denomination.

(2) This section shall not apply to funds from federal sources provided to the state for the express purpose of distribution to non-public education.

Section 7. Nondiscrimination in education.

No religious or partisan test or qualification shall be required of any teacher or student as a condition of admission into any public educational institution. Attendance shall not be required at any religious service. No sectarian tenets shall be advocated in any public educational institution of the state. No person shall be refused admission to any public educational institution on account of sex, race, creed, religion, political beliefs, or national origin.

Section 8. School district trustees.

The supervision and control of schools in each school district shall be vested in a board of trustees to be elected as provided by law.

Section 9. Boards of education.

(1) There is a state board of education composed of the board of regents of higher education and the board of public education. It is responsible for long-range planning, and for coordinating and evaluating policies and programs for the state's educational systems. It shall submit unified budget requests. A tie vote at

any meeting may be broken by the governor, who is an ex officio member of each component board.

(2)

- (a) The government and control of the Montana university system is vested in a board of regents of higher education which shall have full power, responsibility, and authority to supervise, coordinate, manage and control the Montana university system and shall supervise and coordinate other public educational institutions assigned by law.
- (b) The board consists of seven members appointed by the governor, and confirmed by the senate, to overlapping terms, as provided by law. The governor and superintendent of public instruction are ex officio non-voting members of the board.
- (c) The board shall appoint a commissioner of higher education and prescribe his term and duties.
- (d) The funds and appropriations under the control of the board of regents are subject to the same audit provisions as are all other state funds.

(3)

- (a) There is a board of public education to exercise general supervision over the public school system and such other public educational institutions as may be assigned by law. Other duties of the board shall be provided by law.
- (b) The board consists of seven members appointed by the governor, and confirmed by the senate, to overlapping terms as provided by law. The governor, commissioner of higher education and state superintendent of public instruction shall be ex officio non-voting members of the board.

Section 10. State university funds.

The funds of the Montana university system and of all other state institutions of learning, from whatever source accruing, shall forever remain inviolate and sacred to the purpose for which they were dedicated. The various funds shall be respectively invested under such regulations as may be provided by law, and shall be guaranteed by the state against loss or diversion. The interest from such invested funds, together with the rent from leased lands or properties, shall be devoted to the maintenance and perpetuation of the respective institutions.

Section 11. Public land trust, disposition.

(1) All lands of the state that have been or may be granted by congress, or acquired by gift or grant or devise from any person or corporation, shall be public lands of the state. They shall be held in trust for the people, to be disposed of as hereafter

provided, for the respective purposes for which they have been or may be granted, donated or devised.

(2) No such land or any estate or interest therein shall ever be disposed of except in pursuance of general laws providing for such disposition, or until the full market value of the estate or interest disposed of, to be ascertained in such manner as may be provided by law, has been paid or safely secured to the state.

(3) No land which the state holds by grant from the United States which prescribes the manner of disposal and minimum price shall be disposed of except in the manner and for at least the price prescribed without the consent of the United States.

(4) All public land shall be classified by the board of land commissioners in a manner provided by law. Any public land may be exchanged for other land, public or private, which is equal in value and, as closely as possible, equal in area.

Article XI. Local Government

Section 1. Definition.
The term "local government units" includes, but is not limited to, counties and incorporated cities and towns. Other local government units may be established by law.

Section 2. Counties.
The counties of the state are those that exist on the date of ratification of this constitution. No county boundary may be changed or county seat transferred until approved by a majority of those voting on the question in each county affected.

Section 3. Forms of government.
(1) The legislature shall provide methods for governing local government units and procedures for incorporating, classifying, merging, consolidating, and dissolving such units, and altering their boundaries. The legislature shall provide such optional or alternative forms of government that each unit or combination of units may adopt, amend, or abandon an optional or alternative form by a majority of those voting on the question.

(2) One optional form of county government includes, but is not limited to, the election of three county commissioners, a clerk and recorder, a clerk of district court, a county attorney, a sheriff, a treasurer, a surveyor, a county superintendent of schools, an assessor, a coroner, and a public administrator. The terms, qualifications, duties, and compensation of those offices shall be provided by law. The Board of county commissioners may consolidate two or more such offices. The Boards of two or more counties may provide for a joint office and for the election of one official to perform the duties of any such office in those counties.

Section 4. General powers.
(1) A local government unit without self-government powers has the following general powers:

   (a) An incorporated city or town has the powers of a municipal corporation and legislative, administrative, and other powers provided or implied by law.

   (b) A county has legislative, administrative, and other powers provided or implied by law.

   (c) Other local government units have powers provided by law.

(2) The powers of incorporated cities and towns and counties shall be liberally construed.

Section 5. Self-government charters.

(1) The legislature shall provide procedures permitting a local government unit or combination of units to frame, adopt, amend, revise, or abandon a self-government charter with the approval of a majority of those voting on the question. The procedures shall not require approval of a charter by a legislative body.

(2) If the legislature does not provide such procedures by July 1, 1975, they may be established by election either:

   (a) Initiated by petition in the local government unit or combination of units; or

   (b) Called by the governing body of the local government unit or combination of units.

(3) Charter provisions establishing executive, legislative, and administrative structure and organization are superior to statutory provisions.

Section 6. Self-government powers.

A local government unit adopting a self-government charter may exercise any power not prohibited by this constitution, law, or charter. This grant of self-government powers may be extended to other local government units through optional forms of government provided for in section 3.

Section 7. Intergovernmental cooperation.

(1) Unless prohibited by law or charter, a local government unit may

   (a) cooperate in the exercise of any function, power, or responsibility with,

   (b) share the services of any officer or facilities with,

   (c) transfer or delegate any function, power, responsibility, or duty of any officer to one or more other local government units, school districts, the state, or the United States.

(2) The qualified electors of a local government unit may, by initiative or referendum, require it to do so.

Section 8. Initiative and referendum.

The legislature shall extend the initiative and referendum powers reserved to the people by the constitution to the qualified electors of each local government unit.

Section 9. Voter review of local government.

(1) The legislature shall, within four years of the ratification of this constitution, provide procedures requiring each local government unit or combination of units

to review its structure and submit one alternative form of government to the qualified electors at the next general or special election.

(2) The legislature shall require an election in each local government to determine whether a local government will undertake a review procedure once every ten years after the first election. Approval by a majority of those voting in the decennial general election on the question of undertaking a local government review is necessary to mandate the election of a local government study commission. Study commission members shall be elected during any regularly scheduled election in local governments mandating their election.

History: Amd. Const. Amend. No. 6, approved Nov. 7, 1978.

Article XII. Departments And Institutions

Section 1. Agriculture.
(1) The legislature shall provide for a Department of Agriculture and enact laws and provide appropriations to protect, enhance, and develop all agriculture.

(2) Special levies may be made on livestock and on agricultural commodities for disease control and indemnification, predator control, and livestock and commodity inspection, protection, research, and promotion. Revenue derived shall be used solely for the purposes of the levies.

Section 2. Labor.
(1) The legislature shall provide for a Department of Labor and Industry, headed by a Commissioner appointed by the governor and confirmed by the senate.

(2) A maximum period of 8 hours is a regular day's work in all industries and employment except agriculture and stock raising. The legislature may change this maximum period to promote the general welfare.

Section 3. Institutions and assistance.
(1) The state shall establish and support institutions and facilities as the public good may require, including homes which may be necessary and desirable for the care of veterans.

(2) Persons committed to any such institutions shall retain all rights except those necessarily suspended as a condition of commitment. Suspended rights are restored upon termination of the state's responsibility.

(3) The legislature may provide such economic assistance and social and rehabilitative services for those who, by reason of age, infirmities, or misfortune are determined by the legislature to be in need.

(4) The legislature may set eligibility criteria for programs and services, as well as for the duration and level of benefits and services.

History: Amd. Const. Amend. No. 18, approved Nov. 8, 1988.

Section 4. Montana tobacco settlement trust fund.
(1) The legislature shall dedicate not less than two-fifths of any tobacco settlement proceeds received on or after January 1, 2001, to a trust fund, nine-tenths of the interest and income of which may be appropriated. One-tenth of the interest and income derived from the trust fund on or after January 1, 2001, shall be deposited in the trust fund. The principal of the trust fund and one-tenth of the interest and income deposited in the trust fund shall remain forever inviolate unless

appropriated by a vote of two-thirds of the members of each house of the legislature.

(2) Appropriations of the interest, income, or principal from the trust fund shall be used only for tobacco disease prevention programs and state programs providing benefits, services, or coverage that are related to the health care needs of the people of Montana and may not be used for other purposes.

(3) Appropriations of the interest, income, or principal from the trust fund shall not be used to replace state or federal money used to fund tobacco disease prevention programs and state programs that existed on December 31, 1999, providing benefits, services, or coverage of the health care needs of the people of Montana.

History: En. Sec. 1, Const. Amend. No. 35, approved Nov. 7, 2000.

Article XIII. General Provisions

Section 1. Nonmunicipal corporations.
(1) Corporate charters shall be granted, modified, or dissolved only pursuant to general law.

(2) The legislature shall provide protection and education for the people against harmful and unfair practices by either foreign or domestic corporations, individuals, or associations.

(3) The legislature shall pass no law retrospective in its operations which imposes on the people a new liability in respect to transactions or considerations already passed.

Section 2. Consumer counsel.
The legislature shall provide for an office of consumer counsel which shall have the duty of representing consumer interests in hearings before the public service commission or any other successor agency. The legislature shall provide for the funding of the office of consumer counsel by a special tax on the net income or gross revenues of regulated companies.

Section 3. Repealed.
Sec. 1, Const. Amend. No. 16, approved Nov. 4, 1986.

Section 4. Code of ethics.
The legislature shall provide a code of ethics prohibiting conflict between public duty and private interest for members of the legislature and all state and local officers and employees.

Section 5. Exemption laws.
The legislature shall enact liberal homestead and exemption laws.

Section 6. Perpetuities.
No perpetuities shall be allowed except for charitable purposes.

Section 7. Marriage.
Only a marriage between one man and one woman shall be valid or recognized as a marriage in this state.

History: En. Sec. 1, Const. Initiative No. 96, approved Nov. 2, 2004.

Article XIV. Constitutional Revision

Section 1. Constitutional convention.
The legislature, by an affirmative vote of two-thirds of all the members, whether one or more bodies, may at any time submit to the qualified electors the question of whether there shall be an unlimited convention to revise, alter, or amend this constitution.

Section 2. Initiative for constitutional convention.
(1) The people may by initiative petition direct the secretary of state to submit to the qualified electors the question of whether there shall be an unlimited convention to revise, alter, or amend this constitution. The petition shall be signed by at least ten percent of the qualified electors of the state. That number shall include at least ten percent of the qualified electors in each of two-fifths of the legislative districts.

(2) The secretary of state shall certify the filing of the petition in his office and cause the question to be submitted at the next general election.

Section 3. Periodic submission.
If the question of holding a convention is not otherwise submitted during any period of 20 years, it shall be submitted as provided by law at the general election in the twentieth year following the last submission.

Section 4. Call of convention.
If a majority of those voting on the question answer in the affirmative, the legislature shall provide for the calling thereof at its next session. The number of delegates to the convention shall be the same as that of the larger body of the legislature. The qualifications of delegates shall be the same as the highest qualifications required for election to the legislature. The legislature shall determine whether the delegates may be nominated on a partisan or a non-partisan basis. They shall be elected at the same places and in the same districts as are the members of the legislative body determining the number of delegates.

Section 5. Convention expenses.
The legislature shall, in the act calling the convention, designate the day, hour, and place of its meeting, and fix and provide for the pay of its members and officers and the necessary expenses of the convention.

Section 6. Oath, vacancies.
Before proceeding, the delegates shall take the oath provided in this constitution. Vacancies occurring shall be filled in the manner provided for filling vacancies in the legislature if not otherwise provided by law.

Section 7. Convention duties.

The convention shall meet after the election of the delegates and prepare such revisions, alterations, or amendments to the constitution as may be deemed necessary. They shall be submitted to the qualified electors for ratification or rejection as a whole or in separate articles or amendments as determined by the convention at an election appointed by the convention for that purpose not less than two months after adjournment. Unless so submitted and approved by a majority of the electors voting thereon, no such revision, alteration, or amendment shall take effect.

Section 8. Amendment by legislative referendum.

Amendments to this constitution may be proposed by any member of the legislature. If adopted by an affirmative roll call vote of two-thirds of all the members thereof, whether one or more bodies, the proposed amendment shall be submitted to the qualified electors at the next general election. If approved by a majority of the electors voting thereon, the amendment shall become a part of this constitution on the first day of July after certification of the election returns unless the amendment provides otherwise.

Section 9. Amendment by initiative.

(1) The people may also propose constitutional amendments by initiative. Petitions including the full text of the proposed amendment shall be signed by at least ten percent of the qualified electors of the state. That number shall include at least ten percent of the qualified electors in each of at least one-half of the counties.

(2) The petitions shall be filed with the secretary of state. If the petitions are found to have been signed by the required number of electors, the secretary of state shall cause the amendment to be published as provided by law twice each month for two months previous to the next regular state-wide election.

(3) At that election, the proposed amendment shall be submitted to the qualified electors for approval or rejection. If approved by a majority voting thereon, it shall become a part of the constitution effective the first day of July following its approval, unless the amendment provides otherwise.

History: Amd. Const. Amend. No. 37, approved Nov. 5, 2002.

Section 10. Petition signers.

The number of qualified electors required for the filing of any petition provided for in this Article shall be determined by the number of votes cast for the office of governor in the preceding general election.

Section 11. Submission.

If more than one amendment is submitted at the same election, each shall be so prepared and distinguished that it can be voted upon separately.

Signatures.

Done in open convention at the city of Helena, in the state of Montana, this twenty-second day of March, in the year of our Lord one thousand nine hundred and seventy-two.

Leo Graybill, Jr., President
Jean M. Bowman, Secretary
Magnus Aasheim
John H. Anderson, Jr.
Oscar L. Anderson
Harold Arbanas
Franklin Arness
Cedor B. Aronow
William H. Artz
Thomas M. Ask
Betty Babcock
Lloyd Barnard
Grace C. Bates
Don E. Belcher
Ben E. Berg, Jr.
E. M. Berthelson
Chet Blaylock
Virginia H. Blend
Geoffrey L. Brazier
Bruce M. Brown
Daphne Bugbee
William A. Burkhardt
Marjorie Cain
Bob Campbell
Jerome J. Cate
Richard J. Champoux
Lyman W. Choate
Max Conover
C. Louise Cross
Wade J. Dahood
Carl M. Davis
Douglas Delaney
Maurice Driscoll

Dave Drum
Dorothy Eck
Marian S. Erdmann
Leslie Eskildsen
Mark Etchart
James R. Felt
Donald R. Foster
Noel D. Furlong
J. C. Garlington
E. S. Gysler
Otto T. Habedank
Rod Hanson
R. S. Hanson
Gene Harbaugh
Paul K. Harlow
George Harper
Daniel W. Harrington
George B. Heliker
David L. Holland
Arnold W. Jacobsen
George H. James
Torrey B. Johnson
Thomas F. Joyce
A. W. Kamhoot
Robert Lee Kelleher
John H. Leuthold
Jerome T. Loendorf
Peter "Pete" Lorello
Joseph H. McCarvel
Russell C. McDonough
Mike McKeon
Charles B. McNeil
Charles H. Mahoney

Rachell K. Mansfield
Fred J. Martin
J. Mason Melvin
Lyle R. Monroe
Marshall Murray
Robert B. Noble
Richard A. Nutting
Mrs. Thomas Payne
Catherine Pemberton
Donald Rebal
Arlyne E. Reichert
Mrs. Mae Nan Robinson
Richard B. Roeder
George W. Rollins
Miles Romney
Sterling Rygg
Don Scanlin

John M. Schiltz
Henry Siderius
Clark E. Simon
Carman M. Skari
M. Lynn Sparks
Lucile Speer
R. J. Studer, Sr.
Mrs. John Justin (Veronica) Sullivan
William H. Swanberg
John H. Toole
Mrs. Edith M. Van Buskirk
Robert Vermillion
Roger A. Wagner
Jack K. Ward
Margaret S. Warden
Archie O. Wilson
Robert F. Woodmansey

Transition Schedule

Transition Schedule.
The following provisions shall remain part of this Constitution until their terms have been executed. Once each year the attorney general shall review the following provisions and certify to the secretary of state which, if any, have been executed. Any provisions so certified shall thereafter be removed from this Schedule and no longer published as part of this Constitution.

Section 1. Accelerated effective date.
Executed (certified by letter, December 4, 1974).

Section 2. Delayed effective date.
Executed (certified by letter, December 4, 1974).

Section 3. Prospective operation of declaration of rights.
Any rights, procedural or substantive, created for the first time by Article II shall be prospective and not retroactive.

Section 4. Terms of judiciary.
Executed (certified by letter, December 20, 1978).

Section 5. Terms of legislators.
Executed (certified by letter, February 22, 1977).

Section 6. General transition.
(1) The rights and duties of all public bodies shall remain as if this Constitution had not been adopted with the exception of such changes as are contained in this Constitution. All laws, ordinances, regulations, and rules of court not contrary to, or inconsistent with, the provisions of this Constitution shall remain in force, until they shall expire by their own limitation or shall be altered or repealed pursuant to this Constitution.

(2) The validity of all public and private bonds, debts, and contracts, and of all suits, actions, and rights of action, shall continue as if no change had taken place.

(3) Executed (certified by letter, February 22, 1977).

www.ingramcontent.com/pod-product-compliance
Lightning Source LLC
Chambersburg PA
CBHW020628300426
44112CB00010B/1241